THE
WHITE RABBIT
AND OTHER DELIGHTS

THE
WHITE RABBIT
AND OTHER DELIGHTS

EAST TOTEM WEST: A HIPPIE COMPANY, 1967–1969

ALAN BISBORT

Pomegranate Artbooks, San Francisco

Published by Pomegranate Artbooks
Box 6099, Rohnert Park, California 94927

Pomegranate Europe Ltd.
Fullbridge House, Fullbridge
Maldon, Essex CM9 7LE
England

Library of Congress Cataloging-in-Publication Data

Bisbort, Alan, 1953–
        The white rabbit and other delights : East Totem West, a hippie company, 1967–1969 / Alan Bisbort. — 1st ed.
                p.   cm.
                ISBN 0-7649-0011-0 (pbk.)
                1. Posters, American—California—San Francisco. 2. Posters—20th century—California—San Francisco. 3. Social stationery—California—San Francisco. 4. Psychedelic art—California—San Francisco. 5. East Totem West (Firm) I. Title.
        NC1807.U5B55 1996
        741.6'74'0979461—dc20
                                                                                96-26464
                                                                                CIP

Pomegranate Catalog No. A856

Cover design by Marcus Trumble
Book design by Riba Taylor

First Edition
00 99 98 97 96 5 4 3 2 1

Printed in Korea

CONTENTS

PREFACE
by Thomas F. Burke

It must have been early in 1967; 1966 clearly was too soon for me and by 1968 the end was in sight. Despite being the appropriate age (a year and change out of high school) and a local boy to boot, I was strangely oblivious to the kaleidoscopic changes afoot in San Francisco. Working a forty-hour-a-week job (alternating between swing and graveyard shifts) while carrying a full course load at a local college during the day and all the time keeping a wary eye on Vietnam didn't allow much time, I suppose. (Alternative explanation: if one isn't ready to see, it doesn't matter how much or how little time one has—for some, this would become a tiresome mantra.)

I do remember the radios at work being tuned to KMPX (the first free-form FM station) after midnight—the only time one could hear Janis Joplin or the extended-play version of the Doors' "Light My Fire," as daytime radio shows wouldn't touch this stuff. I liked the music, but on those rare occasions when I had time to hear live music (night jobs are a killer in this regard), I ventured out not to the Matrix (Marty Balin's club) or the Longshoremen's Hall, but to the Civic Center Auditorium to hear the likes of Ray Charles and the Beach Boys (the latter, like Charles, now a legend, but then a dividing line of sorts—like the line between drivers of VWs and those with Ford Mustangs). My hair was short then, fringe meant edge and not leather, bells were the province of churches and fire engines, a judgmental attitude toward users of patchouli oil was still in the future, sprouts were what members of my family had called me and others as children, and I drove a Chevrolet (blown V-8, Tijuana tuck-and-roll upholstery, and candy-green metallic paint job, with glass-paks for the right effect. George Lucas take note—my uncle was the Harley dealer in Modesto; I could have been in your movie.).

I was employed by a venerable San Francisco company, then, as now, one of the world's largest financial institutions. Because I was smart (i.e., I could keep both eyes focused) and the job required little except that one pay attention, I soon found myself in charge of a section of what I now understand is known as back office functions in companies whose business it is to buy and sell money (and lives in the passing). Under me was a constantly changing handful of bodies (employers of night people can't be choosey). We worked on the fourth and fifth floors of the company's world headquarters, our desks positioned only a wall and a door away from what seemed like miles and miles of large computers, whose nightly discharge was our daily bread. Those who actually worked in the computer area were the envy of all—they were allowed to turn their radios up to force ten level. For a few months in 1967, or perhaps it was for only a few weeks, an older man (anyone well into his twenties qualified for the description) worked under me. We got along fine, but when he left, I thought no more about him than about any of the dozens I had seen come and go in my short tenure.

Sometime later, probably only a couple of months (the failure to recognize the compression of real time defines for me this period of my life), I took a phone call at work from this fellow. He was on to something, he said (the man was genetically entrepreneurial); could he drop by work and meet with me some evening? He wouldn't reveal what he had going, and even though one doesn't just drop by this particular institution at night for a chat with an employee (security had a lot to say in the matter), I agreed to meet with him. On the appointed night, after a couple of failed attempts to gain entry to the colossus (I ran downstairs every fifteen minutes to check on progress), my man finally talked his way in (guards must have changed shifts) and met up with me, and the two of us—he with a roll of corrugated cardboard under his arm—headed to the company cafeteria on the second floor.

Never having worked a single day shift for this company, I can only speculate about the leveling effect this cafeteria might have had on the hundreds of people who used it. I do know that an empty football field full of formica tables, at two or three o'clock in the morning, with lights dimmed and the stationary fans doing nothing to disperse the lingering aroma of yesterday's spaghetti, is a strange place for two people to meet. But there the two of us were, and Peter, for that was his name, having chosen a table, slit the tape on the corrugated roll. Out spilled a cacophony of color—posters, he said, in response to nothing I had said, for I was saying nothing at all.

From the remove of thirty years, I'm not sure people of a tender age should be allowed an epiphany. Such an experience tends to so harden one's values that his or her flexibility often is later found wanting as life inexorably grows more complicated. Asides aside, there I stood, epiphanizing while Peter talked away. Because I now can reconstruct much of what he said I know some small part of me had to be taking in all the detail, but that night all the big part of me heard was Peter saying, "I need some help with this thing." I must have managed to sputter "no problem" because we were off and running. (Initially, I did my part of the running in what little spare time I had because apparently I had sputtered another "no problem" in response to Peter's "I don't know what I can pay you." Computer printouts were to consume a major part of my waking hours for a while yet.)

Regarding my "cafeteria moment," you must understand that I grew up in households in which nothing hung on the walls (my grandmother's crucifix doesn't count), no sounds could be heard emanating from the record player (we didn't have one), and the only books present were authored by such masters as Harold Robbins; these were carefully hidden by my father (or so he thought) between the slats and box spring of his bed. In short, art, literature, and music had played a negligible part in my life to that point and I had no expectations that this situation would change. In fact, I had paid no attention at all to such matters. Imagine my state, then, as I stood speechless, looking at the posters, struggling to understand how I could have been unaware of the powerful desire lurking within me. In the moment of epiphany I realized I had all the time in the world to wonder about how and why; the goods were right there on the table and that's all that counted. To discover what is desired no sooner than the moment it is handed to you is, I think, called being blessed. Something similar should happen to everyone.

Among the thirty or more posters laid out by Peter that night were a few by a company named East Totem West. Even on a first viewing by my untrained eye, this group of posters seemed radically different from Peter's other offerings (although every one was a joy for me to behold). In retrospect, I am not in the least surprised that my life later became intertwined with the lives of those who were responsible for these posters. But it would be a while yet before we would meet. In the meantime, there would be months of Peter on the road selling posters to

headshops, university bookstores, and even department stores while I labored at the poster distribution company's equivalent of back office functions—packing, shipping, banking, and simple ledger work.

In due course I was entrusted with making the rounds of various suppliers in order to replenish our inventory. By this time I was driving a rather staid Buick Special, its redeeming attribute a large trunk suitable to the transport of boxes of posters (my beloved Chevy had thrown a rod and had to be put down). I can remember a few of those long-ago entrepreneurs: Print Mint, the Texans who ran the Family Dog (Avalon Ballroom), San Francisco Poster Company, Neon Rose (Victor Moscoso), Loren Gillette (who was to achieve fleeting fame for his *Love* poster), Winged Orchard, Berkeley Bonaparte, and so on. All but one were in San Francisco or Berkeley. The exception, East Totem West, was in Mill Valley, a sleepy workingman's village in Marin County across the Golden Gate Bridge and just up the highway from the better-known Sausalito.

Appropriately enough, on my first trip to East Totem West (sometimes just "Totem" or "ETW") I got seriously lost. As I drove around and around and back and forth less than twelve miles from San Francisco, I became acquainted with Strawberry (an unincorporated area just east of Mill Valley), the towns of Belvedere and Tiburon, and large sections of Mill Valley itself, none of which included Throckmorton Avenue, the purported location of East Totem West. As a city kid with attitude, I was damned if I was going to ask anyone for directions. Accustomed to streets that progressed in alphabetical or numerical sequence and that could be counted on to intersect at right angles, I just couldn't get the hang of 150-degree turns, trees (on the streets!) that obscured street signs, discontinuous streets, and streets that changed names without a discernable change of direction.

That day I turned a twenty-minute drive into a three-hour odyssey. When I finally stumbled through the door at 159 Throckmorton, no one said a word about my overdue arrival and I gratefully shelved the excuses I had prepared. I remember thinking that either these people were extremely well brought up or they had a different sense of time (both were true, as it turned out). So there I was, and all of it was there—incense, music, tie-dyed wall hangings, beaded curtains, painted shirts, long hair and beards, fringed leather jackets, bells (to this day Irene denies wearing bells at any time in her life, and she's entitled to remember it just so), bell-bottoms, and the painted bus (as well as some exposed navels).

It was hard for me to take it all in because these people were so personable. They insisted on introducing themselves and learning my name. Even now, nothing about that afternoon seems the least bit corny to me. I was in the land of the White Rabbit and the Cheshire Cat and it had taken only three hours to get there. How could I not come back, again and again?

As 1967 ran its course, I spent more and more of my time hanging at the edge of the energy center of Totem, a house at the end of a dirt road on a hillside in Mill Valley where Joe and Irene McHugh lived. Their home was a beacon for artists, musicians, poets, philosophers, and an assortment of accomplished people who had walked away from old lives and had yet to make a claim on a new profession. This salon at the end of the road appeared to be open twenty-four hours a day, seven days a week. People were coming and going and talking, always talking.

I was considerably younger than most and felt fortunate that my presence was tolerated. I thought I had little to contribute, so I kept my mouth shut and listened. Gradually I came to realize that the alcohol and drugs fueled a goodly amount of bull and absolute nonsense, and that, in short, the scene didn't discriminate. It took me a while to understand that this was Joe's way. It was important to him to get out there and stay out there, and a lot of the others gave an amen to his impulse.

All the bull notwithstanding, three of the regular attendees—Joe McHugh, the host, owner, and publisher; Ron Berkowitz, the business manager; and Nick Nickolds, one of the artists published by East Totem West—became my teachers and their place of business my university. It wasn't long, in fact, before my Harvard-educated teachers at the other university I was attending began to pale in comparison. Eventually I quit school, no longer able to tolerate Economics 1A and the falsely intense discussions of Sartre.

Meanwhile, what some accurately describe as real life went on. That is, I was still working for Peter, and he had a poster distribution company that he hoped would be a springboard to an ongoing concern of some sort. As 1968 began

to take shape, a tension arose between Peter and me that mirrored the larger forces at play in the country. The "revolution" (which many believe took visible form in San Francisco for only a few weeks in the Haight in 1966 before police cleared the streets at the behest of the merchants) was being suborned, leaders were being assassinated, and ships were now departing hourly to Vietnam.

In my little corner of the world I saw Totem begin to falter, its sales dropping under the onslaught of black lights and posters of chimps with diapers sitting on toilets, and I stood helplessly by as Peter took his business (it was his after all, my intense emotional involvement notwithstanding) in a direction that was counter to everything I had come to value. I realize now that I had no call to be surprised, that Peter had never had anything else in mind. At the time, though, I didn't get it, I became an intensely unhappy camper, and I began to examine my options.

I didn't have many, as it turned out. The corporate world was more than willing to take me back (I could still focus both eyes simultaneously); all I had to do was shave my beard and cut my hair. Where did these people get the nerve? Totem, the obvious place for me, but going nowhere at a precipitous pace, was paralyzed by the struggle to provide its core group with weekly checks. Joe and I did try it for a short while on a part-time basis, but there was nothing I could do to change the situation for the better.

In the end I did three things. First, Peter and I declared a truce and I agreed, for a small amount of money, while he relocated to more promising climes, to attend to the straggly and ever fewer pieces of his business with an orderly shutdown in mind. Second, I went to work for the printer who was churning out the blacklight posters (I successfully ignored the implications of this act, not really considering myself beaten). The owner, a veteran trade union man, didn't object to the hair, the dark glasses, and the black trenchcoat. Third, I started a little poster company of my own, the company that would become Pomegranate.

But Joe McHugh, East Totem West, and I were not quite finished. The old labor activist in whose employ I was now earning the lion's share of my meager income, in deciding to become a full-blown capitalist, started his own poster company (the stuff was godawful and his eye for it unerring; the company would prove highly successful and now is a respectable imprint of one of the West Coast's high-profile publishers). Now that my boss was in the business, he couldn't be expected to tolerate a competitor as an employee. So we agreed I would leave (I wasn't about to give up my little company for the privilege of selling blacklight posters).

Reducing my standard of living even further, I decided to try to make it entirely on the proceeds of my own operation. By this time I had built the company from one that fit under the kitchen table in my basement apartment in the Excelsior district of San Francisco (1968) to one proudly inhabiting a 350-square-foot concrete-and-sheet-metal shell in the worn-out shipyard district of Sausalito (1969).

Into my little warehouse cum office, one day in late 1969 or early 1970, strode Joe McHugh. Joe had moved Totem to Sausalito too, and although we were now neighbors we hadn't seen or talked to one another in months. After the preliminaries, Joe announced he was negotiating the sale of East Totem West. This wasn't the first time Joe had tried to get out from under (the last, in fact, had led directly to our recent lack of contact), but I was aghast anyway, not only because of who the potential buyer was, but also because it appeared likely the sale would go through this time.

Now long gone and unlikely to appear in the official histories of the period, Joe's buyer was a prime force behind the commercialization (dumbing down) of the poster market. I've since accepted the fact that it is the companies most intent on commerce that have the money to buy other companies, but that afternoon my shock deepened as I contemplated Totem in the hands of a mere merchant. I asked Joe if he would consider putting Totem quietly to sleep, thereby leaving our pride, emotions, and clearly delineated ownership of cultural history intact. He said he could not, that he had debts to pay.

Because I had no money, it did not immediately occur to me that I might step into the breach. My agitation was such, however, that the idea wasn't long in coming to mind. Nor did it take long to realize. I knew only one person with money, and that was my landlord. He was close to retirement age, a bit dodgy in his business practices, and not a particular favorite of mine. But none of that mattered. It was a desperate moment.

While my landlord had no understanding of what was going on, he clearly was attracted to the action, sensing potential profit. So I wasn't surprised at the ease with which I convinced him to loan me the purchase price in exchange for a fixed interest rate and a promised share in future profits after the loan had been repaid (with loan repayments having a preferential claim on cash receipts—he wasn't stupid). Thus, the deed was done quickly and Joe paid off his printers.

I now had a business partner I wasn't fond of, one hell of a lot of dated, hard-to-sell inventory, and more debt than I had ever thought possible. But I owned East Totem West. For me this was no different from Joe McHugh owning East Totem West. All was well in the world. It would take me more than two years, but I managed to convert the Totem poster and card inventory into enough cash to pay back the loan and interest. The slate now was clean. East Totem West owed no money, it had no inventory, its assets were intangible, and nothing unsavory or contrary to its spirit had been published in its name.

I took this opportunity to effect what I had always believed was the best course and, sometime in 1973, I let Totem go out of business, intact and with an uncompromised history. Ten, or perhaps fifteen, years later, I returned ownership of East Totem West to Joseph McHugh in exchange for a handshake. East Totem West had given me everything and had cost me nothing but a bit of hard work. Moreover, while the values I learned at East Totem West clearly inform Pomegranate, and despite Pomegranate being in many ways the offspring of or successor to East Totem West, it seemed to me inappropriate to bury East Totem West within the confines of Pomegranate. It was only proper that East Totem West reside in the hands of the man who had given it form.

Our coming together again after all these years to put this book together has given me a renewed appreciation of the art that was East Totem West. None of it appears to me to be dated, and I am astonished at the realization that it was all done thirty years ago. I would take as a totem any one of these images over what is currently offered in the United States. Picture it—it's not hard—Michael and Mickey, hand in hand astride a golden arch, sprinkling magic dust and athletic footwear into the insanely adoring crowd below. Can you dig it?

A FLAPPING OF ARMS

Some sage once remarked that if you could remember the 1960s, you probably weren't a part of them. Now, let's see . . . what were we talking about? Oh yes, the 1960s . . .

Chances are that if you're holding this book, and enjoying the visual delights herein, you have your own firsthand memories of that decade. Or, if you are too young or too old to have been a hippie—and are sick of all the hand-me-down memories that pass for baby boomer nostalgia—you're still able to extract a contact high from their psychedelic artifacts. To borrow a hackneyed old sixties saw, we see where you're coming from.

Whatever your perspective, you will be happy to learn that the story of East Totem West, an art publisher, is not the story of the 1960s, or even of that sliver of the sixties fondly recalled as the "Summer of Love." It is the story of one group of disparate yet kindred pilgrims who found themselves in one another's "hippie company" for a brief burst of time (1966 to 1968) in a very fertile place (San Francisco) and then moved on, dispersed like spores from a magical pod, to other callings. The end products of their collaboration are what you hold in your hands. Though they may indeed be emblematic of the decade in which they were created, they're the result of other forces and other times too.

Just as the case has been persuasively made that the 1960s did not really end until 1974—with the resignation of President Nixon—one could argue that the decade actually began as early as April 16, 1943. That's the date Dr. Albert Hoffmann, a chemist working at the Sandoz Lab in Basel, Switzerland, accidentally ingested (absorbed through his fingertips—a wondrous metaphor that!) a derivative from a rye fungus he'd been synthesizing for the previous five years. This was the twenty-fifth in a series of derivatives known collectively as lysergic acid diethylamide, or LSD.

The firsthand account of Hoffmann's experience, preserved in his lab notes, could very well be the first utterance of the 1960s: "As I lay in a dazed condition with eyes closed, there surged up from me a succession of fantastic, rapidly changing imagery of a striking reality and depth, alternating with a vivid, kaleidoscopic play of colors." Of course, it could also be the first utterance of someone who, in 1968, stumbled upon a black-lit wall of East Totem West posters moments after sipping from a spiked wine bottle some friendly stranger had handed him. ("What's in it?" "I don't know . . . do I look like a chemist?")

Dr. Hoffmann's mental rocket fuel fell into many hands between 1943 and 1960. Some were as sinister (CIA) as others were sincere (Aldous Huxley). And some were potentially sensational. Would anyone now believe, for example, that Henry and Clare Boothe Luce, media fomenters of the "hippie threat," took LSD-25 half a dozen times in the late 1950s? Or that, in its May 1957 issue, their *LIFE* magazine ran a laudatory story about "magic mushrooms"?

The messenger who brought LSD to the San Francisco area was Timothy Leary, a clinical psychologist at University of California at Berkeley. As early as 1960 (symbolic, no?), he, Allen Ginsberg, and Peter Orlovsky were taking LSD and heralding a "peace and love movement." From Leary, LSD fell into hundreds of hands, including those of a straightlaced stockbroker named Ron Berkowitz, later to become East Totem West's business manager. "I was with Leary in Mexico in 1963," recalls Berkowitz, "and I took my first LSD down there. At the time, about 2,000 people had taken it. Tim was saying that someday millions would take it. And he was right. LSD changed what we saw. It changed what we thought. A lot of consciousness got changed at the same time."

By 1964, the groundwork was established for the psychedelic revolution that most people in the country wouldn't learn about until late summer of 1967, when Scott McKenzie's hippie-come-lately ballad "San Francisco (Flowers in Your Hair)" topped the Top 40 charts, with a less overt advance warning a year earlier from "California Dreamin'"—lyrics for both songs, not coincidentally, by John Phillips. Starting in 1964, a new type of revolution began shaking the ground as surely as the San Andreas Fault had in 1906. This earthquake didn't bother with

Left to right: Dow Jordan, Ted Barr, Rush McHugh

political, or even intellectual, processes. In fact, it circumvented the entire mechanism of mainstream Western society. This revolt took place on a far deeper—but, paradoxically, less quantifiable—level than at the ballot box, in courthouses, or in classrooms. It came to be known as a revolution in lifestyle, but that does it only partial justice. Sure, it affected the way people lived, but it also changed their perceptions of life itself, propounding what R. D. Laing dubbed "the politics of experience."

By the time the rest of the country got hip to the San Francisco scene, the real revolution was over. Its Bastille Day may have been October 6, 1966—that's when the federal government declared LSD an illegal drug. This, of course, only served to make its taking more secretive and, thus, sacramental. It did not stem the Day-Glo tide in the slightest. LSD in a variety of shapes and colors was readily available—prohibition or no—to anyone with the money or the benefactor: Blue Cheer, Blue Dots, Clear Light, Green Flats, Mr. Natural, Orange Wedge, Owsley (three flavors: white, purple, orange), Purple Barrels, Purple Haze, Sandoz, Sunshine, Windowpane. Other substances that helped fuel the visionary aspects of the time included marijuana (of which 31 different "brands" are recorded), hashish, hash oil, crystal meth, magic mushrooms, peyote, MDA, mescaline, opium, psilocybin. A direct descendent of these potions can be seen in the names of the rock bands that formed and performed in the Bay Area: A Cid Symphony, Blue Cheer, Clear Light, Colours, Crusader Rabbit, Electric Flag, Electric Folk Mind, Emerald Tablet, Euphoria, Evergreen Tangerine, Magnesium Water Lily, Moby Grape, Morning Glory, Orphan Egg, pH Factor Jug Band, Mount Rushmore, Purple Earthquake, Shiva's Headband, Sky Blue, Strawberry Window, Sunshine, and, last but not least, Colossal Pomegranate.

—

Joe McHugh, founder of (and artist for) East Totem West, discovered LSD in 1964, when he was in the army stationed at Fort Knox, Kentucky. He was on the staff of the base's psychiatric department, patrolling the wards atop America's stockpile of gold. He and Bob Hall, his mentor and supervisor, heard about a chemical that the army and the CIA had been experimenting with for years as a possible "truth serum." Truth serum, indeed!

(*There's* a recruitment ploy: Join the Army. Sweep Your Mindfield.) Hall initiated his eager young apprentice— fresh from art school at Lehigh and Rhode Island School of Design—into the psychedelic fold. It is ironic, in hindsight, that this drug—which the Establishment thought would strengthen their hand—became the lubricant for the loosening of society's moorings. What started out as a sinister torture tool had, within a decade, initiated a Dionysian romp into the Aquarian Age. As the city dweller would say, what goes around comes around. As Joe McHugh would say, think about it.

Hall and McHugh ingested a steady diet of alternative viewpoints. New ideas were tested out in therapy sessions and on the drawing board. America's gold reserve seemed like small potatoes compared to the power of the potion they'd uncovered. Soon enough, the main components of East Totem West were in place: art, psychology, metaphysics, and hallucinogens. All that was needed was a nice strip of land in which the magic beanstalk might safely be planted and, of course, the right sort of fertilizer to add to the soil.

That strip of land was Mill Valley, in Marin County, California, a quiet and affordable town (then) at the northern end of the rainbow called the Golden Gate Bridge. The fertilizer would be the crosscurrents of cultural revolution mentioned above, which would sweep in waves across the entire Bay Area.

—

It's easy to get lost rewriting history, especially when the events being considered are nothing short of a social revolution. Because it was a revolution—a time of profound change—the surviving participants, being revolutionaries (at least in their mind's eye or in hindsight, both of which are 20/20), have their own unique perspectives. In other words, not all the canaries are chirping the same tune. To make matters more difficult, many smaller waves had washed over the Bay Area before the big, bright wave of the mid-1960s. These waves were tantamount to prophecies—warnings, some might say. The Beats. The hipsters. The socialists. The freethinkers. The cool comics, performance artists, and free-form jazzers. The Free Speech Movement. The Zen lunatics, serious Buddhists, lotus eaters, and deep ecologists. Henry Miller individualists. Lord Buckley. Dunites. Bohemians.

Although they'd probably protest the notion, each group in its own way influenced the others. It would be disingenuous—and all too easy—to insist that they were unaware of what had come before and what was going on around them. It would, however, be just as easy, and just as wrong, to insist that these different groups used or duped or plagiarized one another. That would have been, if nothing else, physically and biologically impossible. Too much happened in too compressed a period of time for anyone to have consciously manipulated or orchestrated any of it, as much as he or she would have liked to have tried. No, the only thing anyone—including the undercover narcos and cops—could do was to hang on for the long, strange trip.

How turbulent were the underground springs in the Bay Area during the 1960s? A partial list of the underground newspapers being printed simultaneously: *The Berkeley Barb*, *Berkeley Tribe*, *Black Panther Party Paper*, *Bay Guardian*, *Oracle*, *Express-Times*, *Dock of the Bay*. Other periodicals of new arts, literature, and politics being published in the vicinity: *Contact*, *Ramparts*, *Rolling Stone*, *Not Man Apart*, *Psychedelic Review*, *Whole Earth Catalog*. Not to mention the mainstream press, which seemed intrigued if not bemused by the goings-on: the *San Francisco Chronicle*, whose staff included the relatively hip Ralph J. Gleason, yet still printed a typically wrongheaded series titled "I Was a Hippie" during the so-called Summer of Love; *Time* magazine, whose January 6, 1967, issue named the "Now Generation" as "Man of the Year" and whose March 15, 1968, issue borrowed an East Totem West design; and the *Washington Post*, which sent a reporter, Nicholas von Hoffman, who ended up staying a year and writing the best mainstream account of the tidal wave's crest, *We Are the People Our Parents Warned Us Against*.

Then there were certain Bay Area people whose force of personality helped shape events, some of whom had a direct or an indirect effect on the doings of East Totem West: Ken Kesey, Alan Watts, Allen Ginsberg, Lawrence Ferlinghetti, Bill Graham, Chet Helms, Jerry Garcia, Jann Wenner, Grace Slick, Paul Kantner, Bill Ryan, Jim Prior, Michael Bowen, Wilfried Sätty, John Starr Cooke, Diane Brewer, Pirkle Jones, Jean Varda.

Also influential were the galleries and performance spaces in the area: hungry i, Condor Club (where Carol Doda shook her fortified jugs), Longshoremen's Hall, the Fillmore Auditorium, the Avalon Ballroom, Winterland, the Matrix, Blue Unicorn, Coffee and Confusion, Vesuvio, Keystone Korner, Robbie's, Steppenwolf, the No Name bar, Gatsby's, as well as many other unnamed spots taken over briefly by kindred spirits. There were community hangouts like the Psychedelic Shop on Haight Street, which was open just twenty months and which closed on October 6, 1967, during the Funeral for the Hippie. (The sign in the boarded-up window read: "Nebraska Needs You More.") Radio stations: KMPX, the first real FM underground station in the country, beginning on April 7, 1967, when Tom "Big Daddy" Donahue, dubbing Top 40 "a rotting corpse," began presenting an alternative; and KSAN, where Donahue went after being booted from KMPX for insubordination. There were colleges too, always a breeding ground for discontent and creativity: San Francisco State; the University of San Francisco; the University of California, Berkeley; the University of California, Santa Cruz; Stanford University.

So how does one squeeze all that into linear or analytical terms in an introduction to the work of one graphics publishing company—one petal from this enormous flower? Not to be coy or inscrutable, but it can't be done. Suffice it to say, the revolution moved people toward experimentations and alternatives—including the publishing of art—never before tried on such a grand scale.

Besides the aforementioned chemicals, the primary mover of this new way of experiencing was music. The first communal rock "dance" was held on October 16, 1965, at Longshoreman's Hall (near Fisherman's Wharf). Dubbed "A Tribute to Dr. Strange," it was organized by Family Dog Enterprises, the brainchild of Chet Helms, a former Texas preacher who'd brought with him to San Francisco an obscure singer named Janis Joplin. It was a huge success and was followed regularly by such "dance shows" at an old ballroom called the Avalon, which Helms was able to rent inexpensively.

Despite what has been written about the Summer of Love, most of the Bay Area's hip crowd considered the peak of their communal revolt to have been the First Human Be-In (or "A Gathering of Tribes"), held January

14, 1967, on the Polo Grounds of Golden Gate Park. The event was heralded for weeks with press releases like "A new nation has grown inside the robot flesh of the old. . . . Berkeley political activists and the love generation of the Haight-Ashbury will join together."

While such provocative rhetoric had a certain—somewhat limited—appeal, the most unifying tool for organizing the cognoscenti was the poster art that had begun to appear in every shop window, on walls, and on bulletin boards. For the visual artist, it seems, a new challenge was presented by these musical and political doings, with opportunities for the most imaginative among their number. The poster format had suddenly become the medium of choice for the time, with new graphics studios popping up like magic mushrooms after an acid rain. In addition to Family Dog's graphic wing, there was Bill Graham Presents, Berkeley Bonaparte, Neon Rose, The Food, Sparta Graphics, Mouse Studios, Western Front, and East Totem West.

Though five separate posters for the above-mentioned Be-In were circulated, the most famous depicted a Native American on horseback, strumming an electric guitar. Somehow, such striking imagery seemed more trustworthy than TV or newsprint, like a secret language that only the truly enlightened could comprehend.

The poster medium wasn't new, of course. What was new was the attitude taken toward this previously hybrid art form (half commerce, half fine art). The young artists approached the old form with new ideas, visually interpreting an era that, though best known for its booming music scene, was unfolding on all fronts like some enormous explosion of light, sound, and motion, right under their noses.

Nationwide, the so-called poster boom had been ignited earlier that year in New York when someone got the bright idea to blow up Bogart to wall size. The still from *Casablanca*—Rick with shot glass and wounded expression—became a huge seller and was followed by similar big-selling shots of Brando (on motorcycle with Village People–like leather cap), Bardot, Harlow, Belmondo, W. C. Fields, Stokely Carmichael—all the product of Personality Posters. Soon enough, *Life* magazine would prosaically reduce the poster movement to "The Big Poster Hang Up."

"The whole psychedelic rock art thing was true to that great tradition of Lautrec," says Tom Burke, then an East Totem West business partner, now president of Pomegranate Publications. "It announced a specific event on Friday on Haight Street. But East Totem West was really part of a new revolution. Joe McHugh was saying, 'Here's a picture of something that has nothing to do with a bullfight, sports event, or performance, and it's yours for two bucks, and you can put it on the wall.' As for art cards, there was Hallmark and . . . Hallmark. Yes, you could go to a museum and get a lousy reproduction of a Rembrandt painting, but blank art cards as we know them today did not exist. You couldn't get a calendar either, unless it was imprinted by your auto body shop, bank, or insurance agent. There was nothing prior to that, no freestanding mass-produced art. In retrospect, I'd have to say that Totem was pretty funky, but that was its power. It was a new way of looking at things."

By 1967, there were stores in San Francisco (and New York and other urban centers) devoted entirely to the sale of posters, and they were moving as many as 25,000 a month. Posters were sold at all public events too, with enterprising vendors filling the trunks of their cars and setting up makeshift stalls at free music festivals. This is how East Totem West did most of its business at the beginning, and it was as a result of one of these events— the Magic Mountain Fair, "the first and only rock festival on Mount Tamalpais"—that the two people (Tom Burke and Joe McHugh) whose long friendship sparked the publication of this book became aware of one another.

Joe McHugh was adamant about incorporating something besides the fine art tradition into East Totem West's published work. "I always thought what I was doing with posters had something to do with LSD," he says. "The idea of a poster before then was to promote something, a product or an event. I was promoting something too. But it was not a product. It was that acid change of mind. And I felt proud of it, blessed to be part of that whole movement."

In their excellent historical overview of the advent of hallucinogenic drugs, *Acid Dreams: The CIA, LSD and the Sixties Rebellion*, Martin Lee and Bruce Shlain make the point that "while some interesting and highly original works of art have been produced during the acid high,

San Francisco Print Mint poster store, 1967

the creative effects of LSD cannot be measured solely in terms of immediate artistic output. Even more important is the enlargement of vision, the acute awareness of vaster potentials that persist long after the drug has worn off."

East Totem West's art was an attempt to re-create that vision without necessarily having to use the stimulant. Or, as William Burroughs put it, "finding the way back without a chemical guide."

—

The sum total of East Totem West's output seems, in retrospect, relatively humble compared to, say, the prodigious output of psychedelic music graphics being produced across the Golden Gate Bridge or the movie or pop music iconography that found its way onto nearly every adolescent's bedroom wall. The core samples were the 40 or so posters and the 40 greeting cards that are presented herein.

There were also subsidiary products that never quite panned out, including the *Tarot Speaks* Major Arcana mini-poster series and something called "the Flasher," variously described by the principals responsible as a "visual-enhancing color wheel" and "sheer insanity." It's that "sheer insanity" that seems most pertinent now when describing those times. Or rather it seems an appropriate metaphor to use when describing that brief window of time when a "hippie company" could create, produce, and distribute viable and vital artwork, all the while adhering to certain unbending aesthetic and business principles.

East Totem West's principles were not that far removed from those that guided the hand of most Bay Area poster artists—a sense of reverence for the work, a feeling of being part of the fast moving train of cultural history, an honest attempt to define, embrace, and encourage communal impulses. Of course, all of these artists had to eat and pay rent, so the commercial element of the work is undeniable. Yes, they were making money via a capitalist system they were hoping to change, a seeming contradiction in terms. Still, one can sense the tug-of-war—the commercial vs. the sublime—going on within each poster artist's soul just by looking at the final product, which probably explains why psychedelic script was so hard to read. That the

script was the ostensible raison d'etre of the rock posters (after all, the viewer had to know the date, time, and place of the event being advertised) seemed secondary to the artists, as if by obscuring the words they could further blur the line between commercial and fine art and draw more attention to the amazing images they were creating.

East Totem West got around all that simply by offering images for sale. As stated, here's a picture of something that has nothing to do with a bullfight or a sports event or a performance, and it's yours for two bucks, and you can put it on the wall. As for art cards, there were Hallmark and there were . . . East Totem West notecards, which cost 50 cents each.

"As a publisher I felt responsible for putting out a spectrum of what was happening," explains Joe McHugh, "not necessarily what was to everyone's tastes. I felt privileged to have the opportunity, and I took it seriously. This is no knock on the rock poster artists, who did brilliant work, but East Totem West wasn't representing rock music. We were representing a time and a spirit."

These business principles are not the sort that would inspire confidence in corporate CEOs today. They are perhaps best summed up by Joe McHugh in 1970, when he realized that, in trying to keep the company going beyond its time and place, he was going to lose it—and the principles for which it stood—to a group of buzz-cut outsiders to whom he owed a great deal of money. "Unless the energy came from the images, I didn't want to continue supporting the Totem cause," he says. "What with all the novelty stuff coming out on the market—you know, like pigs and rhinos fornicating—the fine art stuff didn't stand a chance."

While it existed, East Totem West was known for paying handsome royalty rates to the artists it hired, and the company itself took care of its employees. The work schedules and rules were relaxed and informal— according to Irene McHugh, "there was no separation between saying now I'm working and now I'm playing." And it would be safe to assume that East Totem West was the only hippie company in the world that had a health insurance plan.

Janet Leigh's poster decor, 1967

"I was excited about what Joe was doing for the artists," says Ron Berkowitz. "It wasn't patronizing at all. And he followed through with it, even when it was obvious East Totem West couldn't continue to exist as a business and employ the number of people it employed for very long. He was trying to find a halfway ground where he could maintain a communal structure with fair play for everyone and still survive as a business. I was supposed to walk the middle road on this."

"Joe was pretty pure about his vision," remembers Tom Burke. "I really believe that his vision of things would not allow him to run a successful business. It was just that the moment came that kept him afloat, and then it passed and he was once again at odds with his culture."

Here, then, is that passing moment known as East Totem West.

A DAY IN THE LIFE

Another part of the East Totem West story began when Joe McHugh met Irene Pshorr. Joe McHugh was born and raised in Ohio, part of a family that proudly traced its lineage to the founding families of the country. Real straight-shooters from the American Midwest, descendants of Benjamin Rush, a signer of the Declaration, for crying out loud. Joe attended Lehigh and the Rhode Island School of Design, where he listened to a lot of Coltrane and Monk, explored modern art, and did everything in his power to break free of his straight-shooting forebears, before being drafted into the army in late 1963.

Irene was born in Munich, into a famous beer-brewing family. ("Like being Miss Schlitz in Milwaukee," she says). She came to the United States at age 5 and was raised and schooled in Scarsdale and Harrison, New York. When it came time to choose a college, she wanted badly to go to the Rhode Island School of Design, which she perceived as a hotbed of rebellion. (Look what it had done to her future husband!) Instead, cooler heads prevailed, and she was bundled off to Sweetbriar, a girl's academy in Lynchburg, Virginia (a town that would later give the world Jerry Falwell). But as these things happen, Irene's best friend at college was Rachel McHugh, Joe's sister, who also seemed determined to test the bounds of family tradition. Irene was instantly captivated by Rachel's strong will and unflinching pursuit of new ideas. (The youngest McHugh brother, Rush, evinced this same streak and would eventually join the staff of East Totem West.)

"Rachel would go to sit-ins in Lynchburg, and she'd stand up for what she believed," Irene recalls. "She also did things that were illegal, at least by the strict rules of Sweetbriar. She was elected to May Court and deliberately showed up in the wrong-color dress, with a professor as her date. That was a wonderful bit of rebelliousness I wasn't able to muster in my own life."

When Joe was discharged from the army in February 1966, he went home to Cleveland and pondered his prospects. Coming up with none, he decided to visit his sister in Virginia. Irene Pshorr was visiting her too.

Irene and Joe McHugh

Joe, Irene, and son Jason, 1969

"There was a certain amount of grace about Joe then," Irene recalls. "He was princely. We stayed up for three days and three nights, and we talked. I had no knowledge of people like Gurdjieff and Ouspensky, and I was fascinated. I also remember even then that I didn't know what the heck he was talking about, but in the space of 10 days I decided to move to California with him. I needed to break away, to bust out from my rigid European roots. So I went back to Germany, closed up shop, sold my car. And when I got back, Joe was ready to leave."

At the risk of sounding nostalgic, that's the way things happened back then. To add to the stereotype, they drove west in a Volkswagen van.

What led them to the Bay Area in August 1966 was Joe's connection to Bob Hall, the psychologist under whom he'd served at Fort Knox. Hall had been transferred to San Francisco, and it seemed only natural for Joe to follow his mentor west. The timing was, of course, fortuitous. The country seemed to tilt toward the Left Coast then, with anything not bolted down to job, family,

Flapping Your Arms Can Be Flying, poster art by Joe McHugh

military-industrial complex, Billy Graham, or Lawrence Welk ending up in California. Oddly, the McHughs weren't additionally lured to San Francisco by the music and art scenes, which were already peaking in 1966. Joe's idea of a good time was sneaking into churches while high to listen to Gregorian chants. He never went through an Elvis rock-and-roll phase. And as Irene sums up her musical tastes, "I remember I'd heard some Bob Dylan and was fascinated with some of it, but I have to say I was in a complete state of naive expectation. I hadn't heard about the cultural revolution that was going on."

When the Hall family settled in Mill Valley—just up the road from Sausalito—Joe and Irene followed suit, their worldly possessions in the vehicle that had brought them across the country. They first rented a little house on Forest Street, in the middle of Mill Valley, which was, back then, a working-class village and an idyllic summer vacation haven for stressed-out San Franciscans. (It's still an idyllic tree-filled "village," but with modest-size homes now going for half a million bucks, the residents are anything but economizing hippies.)

After several trips back and forth to San Francisco, Joe McHugh soon became inspired by the creative energy of the various scenes he was witnessing. First he and Bob Hall, the two LSD and army vets, collaborated on a publishing project that they'd been discussing since their days at Fort Knox. Hall had been fascinated—as only a psychiatrist would be—by the energy Joe McHugh invested in his sketchbooks. The scribbles, drawings, and doodles in these diaries indicated, Hall thought, some deeper meaning. He suggested that the two of them put together a book. He'd write the words, and Joe would supply the drawings. The result was titled *Flapping Your Arms Can Be Flying*. Joe McHugh was pleased enough with the final product that he created his own publishing imprint (Totem) just to put out an edition of it, in a small print run.

The timing was propitious enough to generate interest in the book. Both the San Franciscan Jann Wenner (in *Ramparts*) and Ken Kesey, the Stanford grad who'd become deeply embroiled with the shenanigans of his Merry Pranksters, gave it kind notices. This translated into unexpectedly brisk sales. Joe was happily forced to put out a second printing of *Flapping*.

Apparently the publishing bug was contagious because soon he'd expanded his interest to embrace the poster format that had captured the imaginations of the graphic artists on the other side of the Golden Gate Bridge. Toying with the new (to him) printing process, he produced his first poster, *Love-Space*, the sales of which went right back into the Totem (now changed to East Totem West) kitty to create a second poster, *Aquarian Age*. (See page 19.) Same deal, back into the Cheshire kitty. When, on his third attempt, Joe pulled *White Rabbit* out of the hat, his and Irene's kitchen-table enterprise had become a full-fledged hippie company.

A storefront was found on Throckmorton Street, in the heart of Mill Valley, and East Totem West hung out a shingle. A staff of like-minded souls was assembled: Brian and Betsy Hand, Rush McHugh, Ted Barr, Jim Prior, Doug Weston, Dow and Linda Jordan, Ron Berkowitz, and various benign drifters who did periodic odd jobs. The storefront was conceived of as a gallery space and a retail shop, with most of the company's operations done out of the warehouse space in the back. (Most of the business was mail order.) Though it was soon a thriving member of the local economy, this company of hippies created a spiritual challenge to Mill Valley, a town filled with beer halls and mom-and-pop businesses. With its beaded curtains and suffocating odors of incense and patchouli, with Joe in his fringe jackets and the undeniably exotic-looking Irene in her flowing pink-and-orange robes, East Totem West was, well, an oddity.

Ron Berkowitz, the business manager, says, "A lot of people would take a peek in the doorway and just recoil with horror. Hippies were rare in Mill Valley at the time."

Berkowitz remembers one day taking a break from work at a local bar—a common practice of Totem staffers— just around the corner. He walked right into the middle of a discussion between the old Irish bar owner and the town's police chief. Being 15 years older than the average hippie and capable of "calling on civil training when necessary," Berkowitz was not suspected of having an affiliation with these longhairs infesting the town. "The bartender says, 'Why don't you run these people in?' and the police chief says, just like Andy of Mayberry, 'Hey, Jim, I don't need you talking like that.

I run a quiet town. Those people are quiet. As long as they're quiet, they're welcome. And I don't need to hear any shit from you about it.' I'll never forget it. 'I run a quiet town, and those people are quiet.'"

The hippie company was a walking contradiction from the outset. Irene McHugh says, "I remember trying to run a business in this hyperdemocratic fashion, where everyone had an input. We'd hire people from Synanon to do the packing, and there would always be these meetings where everybody would have their say, trying to have this family-style atmosphere. And I remember thinking at the time that this was no way to run a business."

At any rate, Joe McHugh was quite conscious of his tenuous talents as an entrepreneur, but he wasn't about to ruin anyone's fun. And during its peak, East Totem West was able to carry a large number of people on its back, with fun being a high priority of the staff. (At one point, Joe underwrote the rehearsals of an official East Totem West rock band, a typically quixotic urge.)

"An awful lot of things happened real fast and lasted 18 months to two years," says Joe McHugh. "Bunches of hippies came together all over the Bay Area. We were no different. Then these people got to know each other and began asking questions of each other, and they began to break up. It was the time and the place. Right time, right place. And the same scenario was unfolding all over the Bay Area, in different forms, and probably all over the country. The whole scene got co-opted as quickly as it had come together."

Until then, East Totem West had a pretty good ride.

"The store didn't do any business," says Joe, "which made everyone in town think we were a front for a dope operation. But by August 1967, we were grossing $50,000 a month, just on the sale of posters through mail order and local distributors. People from Wells Fargo and Bank of America suddenly began changing their tunes. I don't know what the other stores in Mill Valley were doing, but they sure as hell weren't doing that kind of money."

What better way to grasp those quicksilver times than by quoting from the brochure East Totem West put out to market their products: "Totem . . . Totem West . . . We are on the West Coast. . . . We are also part of the Western

World. Why Totem? Well, totems are things we identify with ourselves that bring us to us or me to me or I to I. Totem . . . To Tem . . . Tem in conTEMplate . . . and in TEMplate . . . That is, to trace and to replace, and to place ourselves, or as in Totem . . . As in Tote'Em . . . Like Tote 'em bales, that is, an aid to carry ourselves around. And the East, well, somehow or another, many of the concepts running around today are Eastern, that is, come from that part of the world which we point to when the sun rises. . . . That seems kind of silly when we come to think of it because it sets in the West and so East Totem West." The logic of this is as impeccable as it is unsurpassable.

While spontaneity—like this ad copy—was a hallmark of the East Totem West business ethic, the art itself was rooted in much firmer ground. All of the principle artists whose work appeared under the ETW imprint were part of a solid art tradition and brought into this volatile countercultural mix a wealth of worldly experience: Nick and Barbara Nickolds, Joe and Irene McHugh, Wilfried Sätty, Phil Bird, John Hamilton. In short, they didn't exist in some podlike psychedelic vacuum and suddenly just pick up brushes and paint and start drawing psychedelically.

In fact, all of the area's poster artists were accomplished *before* the tidal wave hit in the mid-1960s. They came from various disciplines—fine arts, graphic design, painting, abstract art, calligraphy—and approached the poster genre not in an exploitative way but rather as a way by which they could ride the wave. They were as caught up in the moment as the musicians and the light show designers. And then when it was over, they went on to other artistic pursuits. They didn't view their work as a gimmick or a fad. They saw it as part of their own personal evolution as artists and humans, a continuum of the great roller-coaster ride of Art, as well as a happy way in which they could finally earn a living by their talents. Most of the artists who worked for ETW were ecstatic that they finally could make ends meet with Joe's royalty rates—which were more generous than any of the other poster makers.

When it all inevitably fell apart, after the initial Roman candle–like burst, Joe wasn't particularly saddened or surprised. And he was willing to keep the company up and running, if the art itself warranted the effort. So, after the posters came the notecards (see pages 61–75), which sold well enough to eventually support a run of 60 titles. These were among the first mass-produced and distributed greeting cards that featured original art and were happily devoid of maudlin greetings, another indicator of the new do-it-yourself ethic sweeping the country.

After the notecards came the end, really, although Totem tottered on for several more months. Eventually, to rescue the company from being sacrificed to a group of unscrupulous outsiders, Tom Burke bought East Totem West, mostly to keep the name from being sullied with the schlock these new investors had in mind for it. "Fine art is not a product you can go out and make a market for, and losing Totem in this way was a very serious business to me at age 21," says Burke. "I was a fanatic about the values Totem stood for. All I really knew was that the

reaction I had to the posters at age 18 was still intact, and I couldn't even consider going back to a straight life. At that point, I said I'd sleep on the floor of someone's apartment if it came to it."

To painlessly put the company out of its misery, Burke borrowed $55,000 from his landlord and paid it off in monthly installments of $5,000 for the next 11 months. Joe McHugh was able to pay off his outstanding debts and "walk away with $20,000 in my pocket."

"Its moment had changed and the energy wasn't there, or the interest, to change with the change. And there wasn't anything appealing about the change," says Tom Burke, "but East Totem West's values live on in Pomegranate."

Long story made short.

THE
POSTERS

EAST TOTEM WEST

Mirror photographic montage
by Joe McHugh
23 x 35 in.

More than any other image produced by East Totem West, this poster captures the company in its most hippielike incarnation. Though it never sold terrifically well, this kaleidoscopic group shot of East Totem West artists, staff, and friends was one of its most familiar pieces. It was widely used for promotional purposes, appearing in magazines such as *Ramparts, Evergreen,* even the *New Yorker,* as well as on the walls and windows of the nation's head shops. It was also used to wrap the innovatively designed barrels that were East Totem West's self-defining display cases.

The central image is a photograph taken on a hill above Mill Valley, near the Portuguese cemetery off Tennessee Valley Road. With Mount Tamalpais and blue sky in the background and hippies frolicking around a painted VW bus in the foreground, this image could have gone into that time capsule Carl Sagan prepared for the space probe. Fittingly, the largest figure—the big dude in the outrageous striped trousers and sunglasses—is Wilfried Sätty, though he's seen with an uncharacteristic grin. Also pictured, in varying states of psychedelic rapture, are Joe and Irene McHugh, Rush McHugh, Ron Berkowitz, Brian Hand, Ted Barr, Bob Hall, and other members of the warehouse staff, some of whom had gone through Synanon.

Rush McHugh and Gary
painting the East Totem West bus

The company bought a VW bus to be used for deliveries. When not in use, the bus was parked at Rush's rented cottage across the street from the East Totem West store. Over a period of a few weeks, during lulls in the packing, mailing, and delivering of posters, members of the East Totem West staff—when they weren't out back smoking dope among the redwoods—walked over to Rush's house and applied a few paint strokes to the company bus. Gradually, the quintessentially Totem "magic bus" emerged, as seen in this poster. Most of the work was done by Joe, Rush, Brian, Lynn Gray, Gary, and Lila.

One day, around this same time, Rush was sitting on his front stoop when he noticed someone walk over from the Mill Valley town center to look at the bus. He recognized the person immediately. It was Charles Mingus, the jazz composer and bassist, one of the McHugh heroes. Mingus spent a few moments studying the bus, while Rush remained hopelessly tongue-tied on the stoop. Finally, the jazzman came over and said, "This is one hot piece of material." Rush McHugh considers this his proudest moment as a member of the hippie company.

Brian Hand and Joe McHugh painting the bus

LOVE-SPACE
Poster art by
Joe McHugh
23 x 35 in.

Trained as a studio artist, Joe McHugh had not paid much heed to printing processes or even photography before 1966. In fact, he did not own a camera or see a printing press in operation until that year. That's when he began working on the drawings for *Flapping Your Arms Can Be Flying*, a book collaboration with Bob Hall. Inspired by the unfamiliar technology, McHugh pondered the possibilities. The initial result was *Love-Space*, which ultimately led to the formation of a publishing company, East Totem West.

"The book came out and got a couple of nice, helpful reviews from Ken Kesey and Jann Wenner," he remembers. "So I'm driving around the area trying to sell it out of the backseat of my car. Now it's January 1967, and I decide that to save a lot of money and to make my art, I could make a poster by getting acetates and ink and putting the ink directly on the acetate. Then I can burn those acetates directly into the lithograph plates without any photographs or negatives and put it right on the press and print it. This means, of course, that I won't see what it is until it dries. And that was the mandala called *Love-Space*, the first poster I published. We cut the cost to $300 for a two-color print run of 2,000, just by not using any negatives."

Such were the times that an image created in so ad hoc a fashion began to sell. It sold well enough, in fact, to allow Joe McHugh to take a second crack at the printing process.

"We didn't have the money for color separations to do formal printing, to print posters," says Irene McHugh. "We'd do the separations. We'd create the design. And then we'd hand-do each sheet in black and white . . . the red, the yellow, the blue.

It was an endless process, but that's how all the first posters were created. Then we'd print a few on a shoestring—at Orbit Graphics in San Francisco—load them into the car, and drive all over the Haight peddling them to the stores. When *Love-Space* came out in early 1967, the poster scene was already in full swing. Ours sold, so we went on to the next poster."

AQUARIAN AGE
Poster art by Joe McHugh
23 x 35 in.

With the company East Totem West officially inaugurated by *Love-Space*, Joe McHugh soon returned to Orbit Graphics. This time, he wanted to explore the dimensions of color obtainable by using just black-and-white printing processes. His second poster, the Rorschach-like *Aquarian Age*, resulted. Though not completely happy with it, McHugh felt the experience was a necessary part of his accelerated, and autodidactic, apprenticeship.

According to the East Totem West brochure—printed a year later as a sales tool—*Aquarian Age* was when the company began "to use the printing press rather than be restricted by it."

This same trial-and-error method—cross-fertilized with continued experimentation with psychedelic drugs—would breed Joe McHugh's next poster, *White Rabbit*, the one that put East Totem West on the countercultural map.

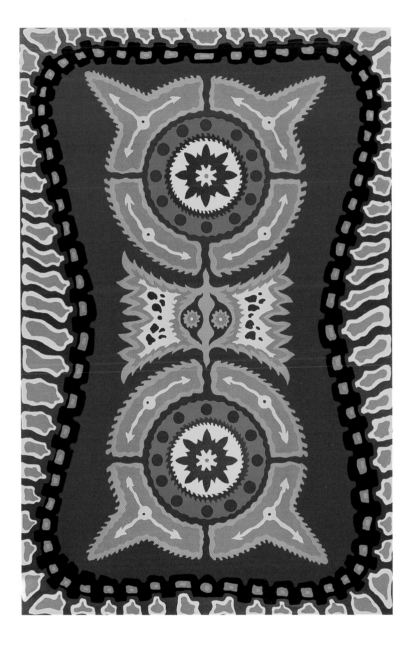

WHITE RABBIT
Poster art by Joe McHugh
23 x 35 in.

WHITE RABBIT

The arrival of *White Rabbit* was tantamount, in the words of Tom Burke, to "hitting a gong and going directly to fame." Single-footedly, this humble hare catapulted East Totem West into a full-fledged business within the space of a few weeks. Hundreds of thousands of this one image were eventually sold, as it became a staple in the decor of every head shop, psychedelic shack, crash pad, and hip salon in the country. Amazingly, Joe McHugh was still employing his hit-or-miss approach to art when he snared *White Rabbit.* More amazingly, he hit the bull's-eye on the first shot. This is further proof of the Zen archer's dictum: you hit the target when you don't aim at it.

"I had it figured for a three-color print, but I could not get across to the printers that that's what I wanted done," says McHugh. "I don't know whether they were saying to themselves, 'Well, he can't afford to do this, so let's not even try.' But I really wanted a three-color image on that poster, instead of this two-color image. And there was no original piece of art to it. The original *White Rabbit* was a bunch of photographic parts that could fit inside an envelope: a rabbit, a bottle, a mushroom. The rest is ink on paper, except for the rabbit, which is the color of the paper it's printed on. The purple is the red and the blue combined, the only two colors we ended up using. Christ, I still can't remember how it got done."

Though various conflicting accounts abound—and contrary to what the Jefferson Airplane may have thought—Joe McHugh had envisaged a series of images based on *Alice in Wonderland* for quite some time. He had even schematically drawn up a list of images to do. They were on the drawing board when the song "White Rabbit" was released by the Jefferson Airplane, which had just replaced its original singer, Signe Anderson, with the singer from a band named the Great Society, Grace Slick. Like many things during those compressed and synchronistic days of early 1967, it seemed perfectly natural for McHugh to pull the rabbit out of his hat. To differentiate his creation from the by-then

popular song, McHugh's message—displayed in retinal-challenging graphics—was "Keep Your Head" rather than Slick's famous exhortation, "Feed your head."

Regardless of the connection—conscious or subconscious—the looking-glass world of Lewis Carroll was a jumping-off point for thousands of amateur acidheads. And *White Rabbit,* the poster, is still a mind-bending image. As the East Totem West brochure put it, "We fell in love, all of us, at first sight. *White Rabbit* is us when we keep our head."

Incidentally, neither the words "feed your head" nor "keep your head" appear in Lewis Carroll's writings. So maybe the argument over whose head was kept or fed first is now moot.

CHESHIRE CAT
Poster art by Joe McHugh
23 x 35 in.

Once again, Joe McHugh prevailed upon the Lewis Carroll touchstone for his *Cheshire Cat*. Upon entering the outer fringes of Wonderland, Alice found a Cheshire Cat perched high in a tree. When she asked, "What sort of people live here?" the cat told her that in one direction lived a Hatter and in the other lived a March Hare.

"Visit either you like," said the Cheshire Cat, smiling. "They're both mad."

Expressing reluctance about mingling with mad people, the innocent Alice—like the fresh-faced runaways who'd begun arriving in San Francisco in large numbers in 1967—was told, "Oh you can't help that. We're all mad here. I'm mad. You're mad."

No more simple and eloquent assessment could have been made about America in the years 1967 to 1969. This probably explains why *Cheshire Cat* was East Totem West's second-biggest-selling poster. The Hatter could have been the Haight and the March Hare could have been Marin County, where many city-heads—already sick of the exploitation of the hippies—were beginning to move, to "mellow out." (Yes, they actually used those words back then.)

CHESHIRE CAT

THE WHITE RABBIT
IN WONDERLAND
Poster art by Joe McHugh
23 x 35 in.

Phase Three of Joe McHugh's fixation with Alice
and her furry friends, *The White Rabbit in Wonderland,* was a direct result of using the printing
process as an artist's tool. Prior to the flowering
of poster art in the Bay Area, the best that artists
could hope for were murky photoreproductions
of their finished works. Though he was still working
through the technical snags, McHugh continued
to believe that the potential of the printing press
had barely been tapped.

"It was a very complicated time," he recalls, "I
always thought what I was doing with posters had
something to do with acid. The idea of a poster
before then was to promote something, a product
or an event. But I was promoting that acid change
of mind."

To promote the acid change of mind—to guide
people there without any chemical at all—McHugh
overprinted two images to create *The White Rabbit
in Wonderland*. He liked it so much he had it shot,
took the negatives, and printed his usual run of
5,000 copies as a poster.

THE WHITE RABBIT IN WONDERLAND

22

PIPE DREAMS

Poster art
by Irene McHugh
23 x 35 in.

Irene McHugh, in her incarnation as Irene Belknap, is one of the most accomplished of the artists who created work for East Totem West, with her magical palate and imagery finding their way into galleries around the world. Even in her earliest attempts, at age 20, she gave evidence of her delicate gifts, as is clear in *Pipe Dreams,* the first poster she created for the company, and *Awakening,* her second poster. Upon viewing a number of East Totem West posters, the young son of a McHugh family friend chose *Pipe Dreams* as his favorite. When asked why, he explained, "It's like looking through a transparent—no, not transparent, a trans*lucent* egg and seeing what's going on inside my head."

PIPE DREAMS

AWAKENING
Poster art by
Irene McHugh
23 x 35 in.

Awakening veered in the thematic direction of
Joe's *Evening Raga* (see page 48), but with a
considerably more delicate touch. Though clearly
derived from sacred Hindu art and architecture,
Awakening's detailed graphic work, the balance
of the images, and the overall aesthetic sense
could have been created only by someone
steeped in the traditions of art, as Irene was.

"THOU ART THAT"
Poster art by Irene McHugh
23 x 35 in.

"Thou Art That" could, in retrospect, serve as a metaphor for the Bay Area at the peak of East Totem West operations. The entire scene—from Big Sur north to Mendocino, in fact—was like a flower within a flower within a flower, the sort of labyrinth M. C. Escher might have created had he regularly ingested LSD-25. The poster's title is taken from India's most sacred book, the *Upanishads* (800 to 500 B.C.). Translated from the Sanskrit, *Tat tvam asi* means "that which is that subtle essence is the self of this All; it is the true; it is the Self. Thou art that, O Svetaketu."

In other words, you are the one who has to figure it all out. Or, as Joe McHugh was fond of saying— after a long enigmatic pause—"Think about it."

By this, her third East Totem West poster, Irene McHugh had hit her stride. She continued to develop as an artist and went on to become the most prolific of the company's notecard artists. Examples of that work can be seen on pages 66–68.

STONE GARDEN
Poster art by Sätty
23 x 35 in.

STONE GARDEN

Of all the artists whose work was published by East Totem West, Wilfried Sätty (1939–1982) went on to become both the most famous—publishing his own books and illustrating the works of Edgar Allan Poe and Bram Stoker's *Dracula*—and the most mysterious. At the time Joe McHugh met him, Sätty—as he signed all of his artwork—was making ends meet as a draftsman for Bay Area Rapid Transit (BART) and an architectural designer on restoration projects. East Totem West was the first publisher willing to print his work commercially. Prior to meeting Joe McHugh, with whom he established a friendly working relationship, Sätty had attempted to market a few homemade posters, but these were blowups of single-image photographs he'd taken, not the montage style that became his signature. And they were decidedly unsuccessful.

Sätty was an anomaly in the innocent Day-Glo world of budding hippiedom. A large, slouching man, Sätty was a brooding presence at any happy gathering, and his art evoked the darker surrealism of fellow German Max Ernst rather than the peace signs and doves of the popular Peter Max. Sätty had reasons aplenty for his grim nature. As a boy in Bremen, he was a witness to the wholesale devastation of his town. During one particularly destructive Allied bombing in World War II, he acquired a sliver of metal shrapnel in his head.

"He was always in pain," remembers Ron Berkowitz, "progressively more pain. I was with him one time when he got one of his legendary headaches. It was so devastating, he just fell on the ground and started screaming, 'Oh God, Oh God.'"

While his posters for East Totem West were suitably playful, they also evinced the darker forces that controlled Sätty's mental landscape. In *Stone Garden*, little mice scuttle happily along the foreground, but in the background eerie tendrils offer a telltale glimpse of the dim mysteries that eventually defined all his work. "We Germans don't see pink elephants," he explained to Berkowitz, "just white mice."

The "white" of the mice is, like Joe McHugh's famous rabbit, the color of the paper on which the poster was printed at Orbit Graphics.

TURN ON YOUR MIND
Poster art by Sätty
23 x 35 in.

In these vertigo-inducing Sätty images, op art collided with a boatload of classical icons. *Turn On Your Mind* and *The Inner Eye* (p. 28) were about as close to the "hippie philosophy" as a misfit like Sätty could come. And yet, despite his brooding manner, he was an ambitious artist who cultivated a wide circle of friends (or, rather, fellow revelers), as well as whatever ways and means might be used to unlock the mind's constrictions.

"Hitler's dictatorship was based on a communications-industrial trip," he told *Rolling Stone* in the late 1960s. "Now we are into a communications-electronic trip and the implications are much more total—it can turn us into an entirely mindless society. We must find a way to overcome that."

His primary means of overcoming mindlessness was to strengthen his inner eye. He also served as the inner-optometrist for an ever-expanding clique that showed up on his North Beach doorstep. It was there that he shared a space with fellow artist David Singer, who would go on to create some of the most interesting of Bill Graham's rock posters. Together they dug out the basement, turning it into a dark, plush, art-filled room that has been variously described as "a cave" and "a dungeon with oriental rugs, filled with strange, whispering people." At any rate, this salon would soon be attracting the Bay Area avant-garde, musicians (the Avalon was just around the corner), and actors like Michael Douglas and Anjelica Huston. It had a dirt floor, it was lit by candles, and the only way in and out was via a ladder through the floor of the house itself. Sadly—some might say inevitably—Sätty would take a fatal spill from this very same ladder in 1982.

TURN ON YOUR MIND

THE INNER EYE
Poster art by Sätty
23 x 35 in.

LISTEN SLEEP DREAM
Poster art by Sätty
23 x 35 in.

The complexity of Sätty's later work—especially his
exquisite book *The Cosmic Bicycle* (1972)—can
also be seen in his 1968 poster *Listen Sleep Dream*.
Like many of his landscapes, this image suggests
the residual effects of his childhood traumas in war-
torn Nazi Germany. He described the ambivalence
of his boyhood in Bremen to *Rolling Stone*: "The city
had been reduced to a wasteland, but for a child it
was an enormous playground." His favorite
"playhouse" was a half-demolished medieval
clocktower, which became a recurrent image in his
work. The destruction of civilization is a whispering
presence on the fringe of any of Sätty's work.

"He carried the weight of World War II on his
shoulders," says Joe McHugh. "He was an intense
but bothered soul, and a hard guy to be around
sometimes—never a light moment with Sätty. But he
was amazingly prolific. I couldn't afford to do all he
wanted to do."

By 1971, Sätty had three separate one-person
shows in San Francisco and two books published
and was widely known throughout the world.

LISTEN SLEEP DREAM

Ass id EgG
Poster art by
Nick Nickolds
23 x 28 in.

Joe and Irene McHugh met Nick and Barbara Nickolds through their paintings, which the McHughs saw for the first time at Diane Brewer's gallery in Sausalito (upstairs from the No Name bar). The Nickoldses' work reflected a recent visit they had made to Mexico, and the connection was immediate and powerful. Nick Nickolds was already a well-established painter, considerably older than Joe and Irene McHugh, with a colorful past as a poet, philosopher, and labor organizer to match. He was also well known around Sausalito, a funky bay-fronting village (then), with its own celebrated bohemian past and present. Sausalito was, in fact, the center of a cultural revolution of its own in the 1960s that was oblivious—and in some ways diametrically opposed—to the hippie stampede on the other end of the Golden Gate Bridge, which loomed over the town's shoulders. Theirs was an older, more established scene, with connections to the Beats, Henry Miller (via Jean Varda), Lord Buckley, and the Zen circle of Alan Watts, the charismatic Brit who'd made Eastern religion comprehensible to a Western audience and who lived on a houseboat in the legendary Gate 5 community.

It was inevitable, perhaps, that the Nickoldses would cross paths with the younger McHughs. That it was sooner rather than later is just another fitting piece of the puzzle that defines those furiously eventful times. Nick Nickolds walked into the East Totem West storefront in Mill Valley to offer some drawings he'd done for consideration as poster art. Joe McHugh liked them immediately and printed some, and promptly paid Nick Nickolds Totem's generous royalties. Nickolds was so pleased with the unusual but lucrative arrangement that he continued to produce work for East Totem West. Though well regarded by collectors, Nickolds was living hand to mouth. "He'd have to go look at his work at the framers'," Joe McHugh recalls, "because he couldn't pay for the frames" and therefore couldn't get his paintings back from them.

ASS ID EGG

Ass Id Egg is the best known of Nick Nickolds's many East Totem West images, and arguably his most unusual. *Ass Id Egg* was his first attempt at using montage, combining his unerring eye for detailed imagery with his painter's virtuosity. The "ass" was borrowed from another photographer's work, and the "egg" was a popular and potent symbol for many Bay Area artists, though Nickolds gave it a sardonic spin. He served the entire concoction in a whirling dish of primal urges on the open-all-night surrealistic pillow of the "id."

Or, according to the East Totem West brochure, "All move against and with one another to take us into our own infinity through the eye of our beloved woman, and the strong and stately arches of our being."

Red animA
Poster art by
Nick Nickolds
22 x 33½ in.

In the 1960s, the psychology of C. G. Jung was as
thoroughly explored by countercultural pilgrims as
the Zen writings of Sausalito's Alan Watts and the
mescal-induced musings of Berkeley-based Carlos
Castaneda. Among Jung's more persuasive theories
were the competing concepts of animus and anima,
the male and the female principles. Using photographic montage and Joe McHugh's penchant for
printing experimentation, Nick Nickolds explored
Jungian territory in *Red Anima*, *Stoned Touch* (p. 32),
and *Masked Bath* (p. 33). All three images resemble
friendly brawls between the sexes, or perhaps anti-
Freudian free-for-alls set somewhere in the deepest
recesses of the unconscious mind. Nickolds was the
only Totem artist at the time who had the scholarly
frame of reference within which to adequately
explore such ambitious themes.

RED ANIMA

STONED TOUCH
Poster art by Nick Nickolds
22 x 33½ in.

MASKED BATH
Poster art by Nick Nickolds
22 x 33½ in.

AMERICAN SHAKTI

Poster art by Nick Nickolds
22 x 30 in.

Though Nick Nickolds is listed as the artist of *American Shakti*, it was actually a collaboration between Nick, Joe McHugh, and a San Francisco printer named Jack Kaus (of the company Hogan and Kaus). As described in the Totem brochure, "Joe and Nick worked from an original collage of Nick's." Combining Nickolds's solid image with a shuffling of the color separations, they turned the picture "upside down and backwards, using the yellow as black, black as blue, red as yellow, blue as red, and red as red."

The result was the most precise embodiment of East Totem West's philosophy, underscored by the company name. "Shakti"—according to Yogananda, whose best-selling book *Autobiography of a Yogi* had begun to leave its mark on sixties' spiritual currents and who'd set up a home base in the southern California town of Encinitas—is "the activating force that makes possible the infinite unfoldments of the cosmos." It is a force that transcends religions, taking the same "trinitarian reality" as the Christian Holy Trinity. It's a measure of Joe McHugh and Nick Nickolds's seriousness of intent that they were trying to re-create the Shakti experience through a two-dimensional, purely visual medium using only color.

HARI KRISHNA
Poster art by
Barbara Kahn Nickolds
14 x 18¾ in.

While not one of the biggest-selling images East Totem West printed in poster or card format, *Hari Krishna*—created by Barbara Nickolds—may have been seen by more Americans than all Totem's images combined. The reason: *Time* magazine, in its March 15, 1968, issue appropriated the poster for a cover story on the Joffrey Ballet. Actually, *Time* used only the border of the poster, artfully cropping out any of the Eastern religious elements and rendering the title illegible, replacing them with gyrating, tightly clad dancers. Presumably, the intended effect was to suggest that the *Time-Life* juggernaut was "with it." And if this wasn't enough to convince people that the cultural revolution was being co-opted, about the same time Nelson Rockefeller had borrowed psychedelic design and graphics for his campaign posters.

More pertinently, *Time* offered no credit line to either Barbara Nickolds or East Totem West. While East Totem West pondered a copyright violation claim against Mr. Luce, the company had a small skeleton of their own rattling about the closet.

"We wrote *Time* asking for a follow-up mention," explains Joe McHugh. "We said, 'You used our border on your cover.' But they ignored us completely. In the meantime, we published one of Nick's collages for which he'd used part of a *Life* magazine photographer's famous images. So we didn't press the matter because they could come right back at us."

Besides, a certain amount of satisfaction was engendered by the appearance of even a portion of an East Totem West poster on the cover of America's most widely distributed mainstream news magazine. Call it a subtle subversive act.

As for the religious message of *Hari Krishna*, no one in East Totem West was, ever had been, or ever would become a member of the Krishna clan—not that they had anything against those cheerfully beatific souls. The message of the poster was one of general spiritual affirmation. According to the East Totem West brochure, it was "too religious to translate in any other way than looking at what Barbara Nickolds has given us."

Janis Joplin with her car, painted by John Hamilton
Photograph copyright © Jim Marshall

TOTEM I

Poster art by
John Hamilton
23 x 35 in.

Like the Nickoldses, John Hamilton had shown his work at the Moonstone and Horizon galleries in Sausalito. He was well regarded, with a collector back East who bought many of his paintings and drawings. About the time he came to the attention of East Totem West, Hamilton had gained nation-wide notoriety for a commission from Janis Joplin—she hired him to paint her car, a Karmann Ghia. He did such a wild and beautiful job of it that it was featured in the media across the country as yet another example of the fluourescent greening of America.

Hamilton's *Totem I* was a careful study in black and white. He used symmetrical forms inspired by the artwork of Pacific Northwest Indian tribes as seen on their totem poles and housefronts. But in place of the Kwakiutl or Haida falcon, eagle, or turtle figures, Hamilton appropriated the religious symbolism of Eastern faiths. Though he used some Hindu and Buddhist imagery, and even the meticulous calligraphy of Moslem texts, he retained the formal structure of the Native American totem pole. This fit in nicely with what Joe McHugh intended when he chose his company's name. "I wanted to publish graphic icons that would use a mixture of Eastern and Western philosophy," says Joe McHugh. "The poster or the card would be the totem with which to accomplish this."

TOTEM I

THE TEMPTATION OF EVE

Poster art by John Hamilton
23 x 35 in.

Hamilton took the Hindu graphical elements to their colorful extremes in *The Temptation of Eve*, with the Bible's earliest heroine being cast as a dancing Kama Sutran temptress. What would Jesse Helms or Pat Robertson think of this?

By all accounts, Hamilton was an easygoing man with vast artistic talents. Today he is still painting, mostly beautiful desert landscapes. He makes his living as a vagabond carpenter, residing in a truck with a house mounted on it. When he gets enough money together, he disappears into the desert and paints, still a torchbearer of the East Totem West spirit.

THE TEMPTATION OF EVE

CRY FREEDOM
Poster art by an anonymous
Spec/4 serving in Vietnam
23 x 35 in.

Cry Freedom was, in many ways, the most unusual poster East Totem West produced. First and foremost, it was blatantly—even brutally—political, as topical as the newspaper headlines used in the design. Prior to this, Totem politics had been anything but incendiary or even radical. It could perhaps be summed up by other poster titles like *Turn On Your Mind* or the message of *White Rabbit,* "Keep Your Head."

Cry Freedom came in over the transom, supplied by a Spec/4 (army personnel) who'd been wounded in Vietnam. While undeniably a powerful and brave poster, and based on firsthand knowledge of a war that was further widening the rift between young and old in America, *Cry Freedom* did not sell.

"A lot of people and store managers ordered *Cry Freedom,*" recalls Ron Berkowitz, "then they sent it back when they read it."

"*Cry Freedom* marked the end for me," says Tom Burke, who had been hired by then as an assistant to Joe McHugh, "a brilliant end."

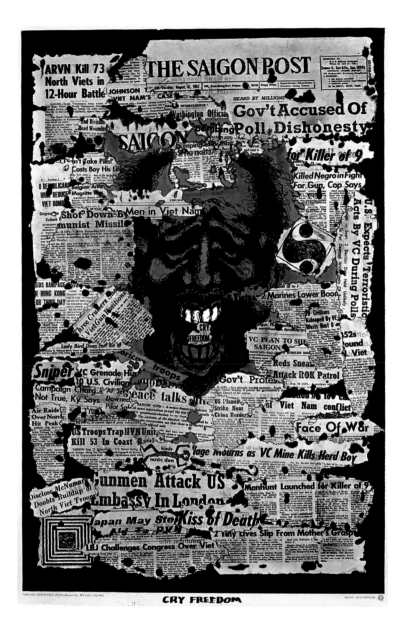

CRY FREEDOM

Mushroom lady

Poster art by anonymous
23 x 23 in.

While listed in the catalog as an anonymous work, *Mushroom Lady* was a collaboration of several people, none of whom wanted to take credit. The central image is a photograph of a Mexican woman, which is then superimposed on an image of a magic mushroom. According to the East Totem West staffer who acquired the photograph from a friend, "She had a look on her face that struck a chord in me. A very deep expression." This same quality was intended to be conveyed by the final work *Mushroom Lady*—according to the catalog, "She was the eternal woman who has been gathering mushrooms for friends and neighbors at least for her eternity."

But, in keeping with the East Totem West spirit, Joe and Rush McHugh added some background painterly effects, which were redolent of the popular light shows at Bay Area rock venues like Winterland and the Avalon Ballroom, and some of which Joe himself had begun to stage for private parties. While the overall effect reflected the hippie zeitgeist, it angered some of the staff, who thought it "robbed the woman of her integrity." Joe, however, would insist, "She smiles at us through the camera's eye, knowing that it, too, is just another mirror."

Perhaps corroborating the McHughs' confidence in the final image, *Mushroom Lady* was one of only four images selected for inclusion in the seminal publication *The Great Poster Trip: Art Eureka* (1968). Sales were relatively brisk, too.

The artist who originally designed the image (who shall remain nameless) wanted a diamond shape, rather than the regular East Totem West square. So Joe and Rush turned the paper at an angle when they ran it through the press, and then (for good measure, perhaps) they ran it through a second time, this time straight up, so that the result was a double image, unique for its time.

LADY SPOON
Poster art by Phil Bird
23 x 35 in.

Phil Bird was a San Francisco artist known for the
meticulous detail and elegant design of his work.
On his first visit to Bird's Mission District studio, Joe
McHugh was amazed by the artist's unorthodox
methods of composing his enormous images. An
entire wall of Bird's studio was covered with four-
inch-square ink drawings. He stood before these
hundreds of square sections like a conductor in
front of an orchestra and composed his works by
combining whichever sections caught his eye at
that particular moment.

All three of the posters he designed for East Totem
West—*Lady Spoon*, *Morning Star* (p. 42) and *Be
Good to Yourself at Least Once a Day* (p. 43)—were
the kaleidoscopic results of several Bird wall sessions.

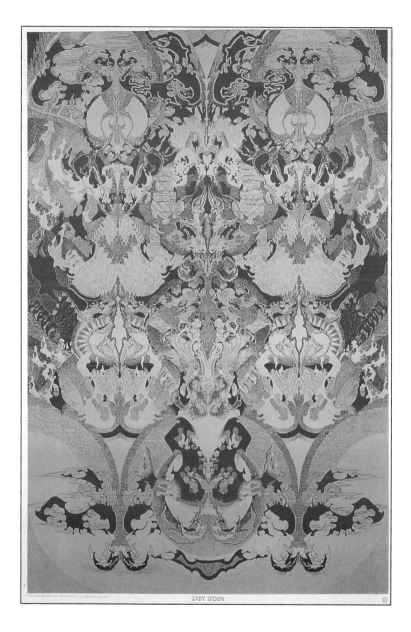

LADY SPOON

MORNING STAR
Poster art by Phil Bird
23 x 35 in.

BE GOOD TO YOURSELF
AT LEAST ONCE A DAY
Poster art by Phil Bird
23 x 35 in.

FLAPPING YOUR ARMS
CAN BE FLYING
Poster art by Joe McHugh
17½ x 22½ in.

Flapping Your Arms Can Be Flying was the title of the little book that got the big Totem ball rolling for the McHughs. Predating the birth of their poster enterprise (but published under the Totem imprint), the book sold well. Undoubtedly, part of the appeal of the book was the arresting cover art that Joe had created. This was the first two-color printing he'd ever done. The green-on-red design quite naturally lent itself to the large poster format, and after a few of the other poster titles were published and distributed, this one was sent from the Totem nest. It flew just fine.

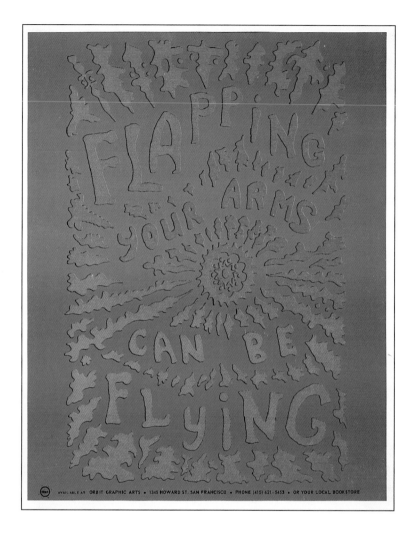

FLIGHT PATTERNS
Poster art by Joe McHugh
23 x 35 in.

Flight Patterns was the extended version of *Flapping Your Arms Can Be Flying*. Think of it in the same light as the Iron Butterfly's long version of "In-A-Gadda-Da-Vida" vs. their more radio-friendly version that became a hit single. Or, if you don't like that metaphor, try another Los Angeles band's long vs. short takes of "Light My Fire." It's all the same airspace.

Way-showeR

Poster art by John Starr Cooke
23 x 33½ in.

One of the most mysterious figures on the fringe of psychedelic subculture was a man named John Starr Cooke. His roots go back to the earliest experimentation with both hallucinogens and spiritual seeking. It's perhaps an indication of his inscrutability and self-mythologizing that his name was routinely misspelled on East Totem West publications.

Cooke began his long, strange trip as a rich boy from an influential California family. One of the heirs to the Cook Travel Agency fortunes, he lived part of the time, even during some of his drug-reveling days, in the Cooke family mansion, a huge old spread in Kentfield, located in central Marin County. With a trust fund at his disposal, he traveled widely, seeking out spiritual guides along the way. Unbeknownst to anyone at East Totem West, Cooke was alleged to have contacts at the CIA, as well as an intimate connection to L. Ron Hubbard, the dictatorial founder of the Church of Scientology. One thing is known for certain: while on a trip to Algiers in the late 1950s, Cooke contracted polio. He liked to suggest that he was "hexed by an African voodoo expert."

Permanently wheelchair-bound, Cooke moved to Carmel, where he hung out a shingle as a psychic-for-hire. He claims to have taken LSD every day for two years while conducting intensive research on the tarot with a group of devotees. Using the results of a series of Ouija readings conducted in 1962 and 1963, he re-imagined the 22 Major Arcana of the tarot deck "for the Aquarian Age." Untrained as an artist, Cooke painted what was revealed to him by instinct. One of his protégés, Michael Bowen, went on to gain renown as an artist at the *Oracle* and become a driving force behind the First Human Be-In. In 1968, Bowen brought the tarot deck that Cooke designed to the attention of Joe McHugh. McHugh decided to test-publish one of the Major Arcana, *Way-Shower*, as a poster. He eventually sank most of the company's capital into printing the entire deck as mini-posters, in the ill-fated *Tarot Speaks* project. "I really felt at the time that all artists should interpret the tarot," Joe McHugh says. "When

I saw these cards, I could tell that the person who painted them was not an artist." To further confuse matters, in *The Great Poster Trip: Art Eureka*, *Way-Shower* was credited to Cooke, Bowen, and someone named Fortner. Nonetheless, *Way-Shower* is strong evidence of the spiritual currents that flowed from all corners of the globe into the Bay Area at the time. Besides his work for the *Oracle*, Bowen designed notecards for East Totem West and illustrated Tim Leary's book on the I Ching, *Psychedelic Prayers*. Cooke died in 1976 in Mexico, where he'd been directing a hard-core group of devotees known as the Psychedelic Rangers.

INDIAN ELEPHANT
Poster art by Robert Moon
23 x 35 in.

The childlike, cut-and-paste quality of *Indian Elephant* was fully intended by its artist, blessed with the fortuitously cosmic name Bob Moon. While this was Moon's only poster for East Totem West, all of the company's familiar elements are in place: psychology (the Rorschach effects), psychedelics (kaleidoscopic colors), ancient philosophy (East meets West) and offbeat printing technique. The circular images also fit right in to the circular logic of the company's brochure: "*Indian Elephant*, lovely to look at but more fun to play with, a toy but not a toy, something to enable us to use our hands and lead us into creation of our own, a first easy step in learning to do rather than to look, because it does take doing to be, and being is what we are doing."

In other words, anyone had the potential to create East Totem West posters. All you needed was the right time and the right frame of mind.

INDIAN ELEPHANT

EVENING RAGA

Poster art by Joe McHugh
23 x 35 in.

In the mind's eye of all self-respecting hippies, the culture of India was the (Cheshire?) cat's pajamas. It all started when the Beatles, the Stones, and even the Beach Boys drifted off to the subcontinent to sit at the feet of this or that bearded guru. As early as 1965, India's most celebrated musician, Ravi Shankar, gave sitar lessons to George Harrison, and the instrument's mind-bending drone was heard on *Rubber Soul.* Shankar became a fixture on the campus and festival circuit (including 1967's Monterey Pop Festival, just down the road from the Bay Area), even inspiring a brief hybrid known as "raga rock." (*Raga,* a Sanskrit word for "color tone," is more commonly used to describe the melodic formulas of Hindu music, as practiced by Shankar.)

The simultaneous interest in Eastern religion and philosophy brought the sacred art and architecture of India into the visual lexicon of American poster artists as well. Joe McHugh borrowed a number of Hindu sculptural elements (as well as sneaking in a few Buddhas) for his photographic montage *Evening Raga.* The same hypnotic—and somewhat frightening—quality of a Shankar raga is evident here, with the layered shape of the image exploding from a central mandala-like point. The Totem take on *Evening Raga,* as described in the company brochure, was that it was "attempting in its way to bring us into the center of the oncoming night, with faith that day will return and that the night too holds our beauty and gentles it if we accept our fear, and don't try to run because of it."

EVENING RAGA

Magic mandalA

Poster art by Joe McHugh
30 x 40 in.

The mandala was a popular mode of expression for East Totem West artists, particularly in the notecard line. Like many things in the late 1960s, it was borrowed from Eastern religious iconography. *Mandala* has a threefold meaning that fit in with the company's guiding philosophy.

First, in Tibetan religious ceremonies, a mandala is meticulously created over a period of days with sands of different colors. Then, in a few seconds, the gorgeous mandala is swept away with a whisk broom, symbolically disposing of worldly attachments. Second, as a work of art, a mandala is a concentric ordering of the cosmos, often using geometric shapes splayed outward to the edge of the canvas. Finally, in psychology, Carl Jung—whose post-Freudian theories were gaining adherents in progressive hippie circles—adopted the term "mandala" to represent the effort to reunify the self. Since one of Joe McHugh's goals was to unify spiritual, artistic, and psychological impulses, it is only natural that he would produce the kaleidoscopic, Rorschach-like *Magic Mandala*.

THE OVERPRINTS

Joe McHugh, Nick Nickolds, and Sätty shared an interest in the possibilities of the offset printing press as a creative, rather than merely reflective, tool. Toward that end, a great deal of time was spent experimenting on press at Orbit Graphics, where East Totem West printed its posters. Led by McHugh, the artists printed negatives backward and upside down; they printed the red film with blue ink, the yellow film with black; they overprinted existing posters using one or more of the negatives from the poster currently on press. Some of the resulting images became part of ETW's regular poster line (*White Rabbit in Wonderland,* for example). Over time, hundreds of images—many printed only once—were created by on-press experimentation. Reproduced on the following pages are several examples (from the small number that survive) of this most interesting archive.

WHITE RABBIT

WHITE RABBIT

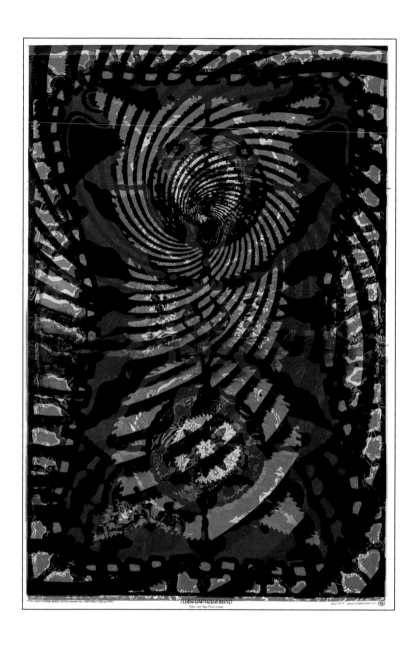

EVENING RAGA

THE NOTECARDS

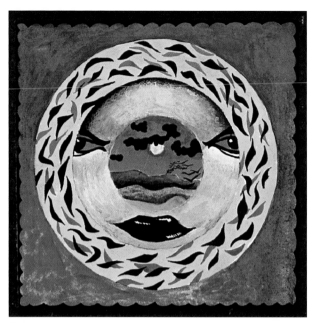

MOON BIRTH MANDALA
Ted Barr

SUN LEAVES MANDALA
Ted Barr

SILENCE
Michael Bowen

I dreaM
Diane Brewer

WonderlanD
Diane Brewer

I love yoU
Susan Kelk Cervantes

MiracleS
Susan Kelk Cervantes

I LOVE yoU
Card interior design by Joe and Irene McHugh

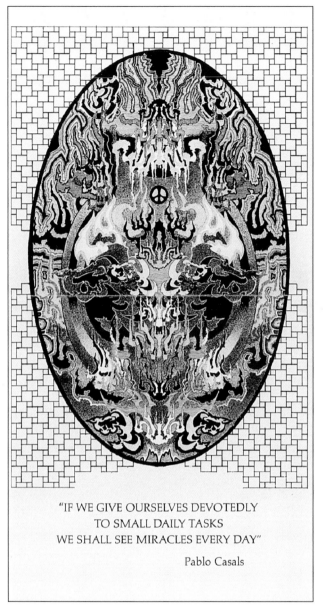

"IF WE GIVE OURSELVES DEVOTEDLY
TO SMALL DAILY TASKS
WE SHALL SEE MIRACLES EVERY DAY"

Pablo Casals

MiracleS
Card interior design by Phil Bird

WHERE HAS THE BOWL WEEVEL GONE
John Hamilton

TO MY LOVED ONES
John Hamilton

THE RECEIVER
John Hamilton

DAPHNE AND CLOE
Irene McHugh

DREAMS
Irene McHugh

LEDA AND THE SWAN
Irene McHugh

SILVER BELLS AND COCKEL SHELLS
Irene McHugh

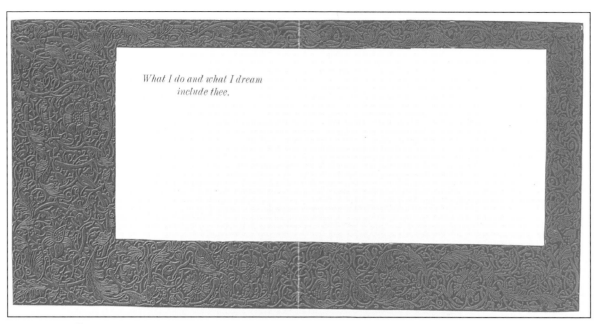

What I do and what I dream include thee.

DreamS
Card interior design by Joe and Irene McHugh

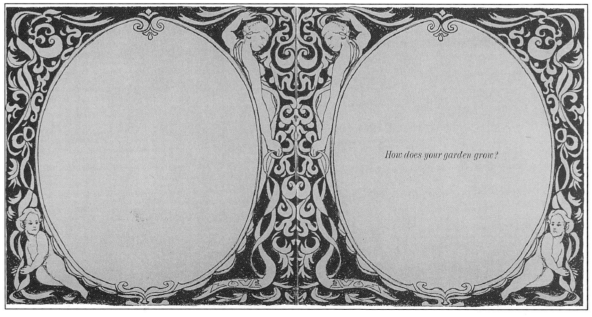

How does your garden grow?

SILVER BELLS AND COCKEL SHELLS
Card interior design by Irene McHugh

LOVE OF TWO AS ONE MANDALA
Irene McHugh

MOON-FIRE MANDALA
Irene McHugh

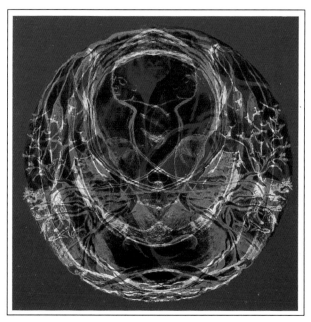

REMEMBRANCES
Irene McHugh

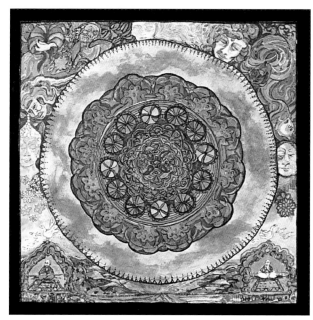

WINTER SOLSTICE MANDALA
Irene McHugh

FlighT
Joe McHugh

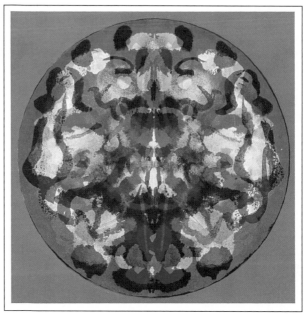

See yourselF
Joe McHugh

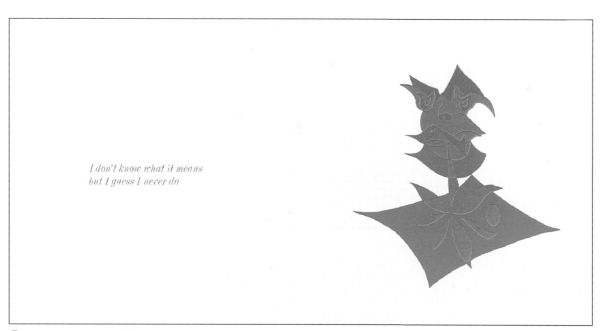

*I don't know what it means
but I guess I never do*

See yourselF
Card interior design by Joe McHugh

ECSTASY OF GRACE
Joe McHugh

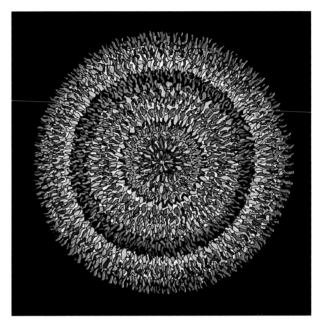

MIDNIGHT SUN MANDALA
Joe McHugh

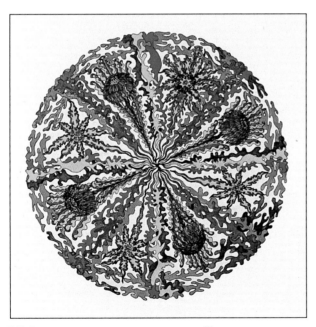

WOOD ROSE MANDALA
Rush McHugh

BHAGAVAD-GITA MANDALA
Barbara Khan Nickolds

BODI treE
Barbara Khan Nickolds

EGYPTIAN eyE
Barbara Khan Nickolds

JOY ENTERS JOY MANDALA
Barbara Khan Nickolds

YOGA OF KNOWLEDGE MANDALA
Barbara Khan Nickolds

ANIMA OCCULTA
Nick Nickolds

PERSONA SUB-AMERICANA
Nick Nickolds

THE PEYOTE ALCHEMIST
Nick Nickolds

TEHUTI IN CONSTANT TWILIGHT
Nick Nickolds

ETERNITY
Sätty

SUNSHINE
Sätty

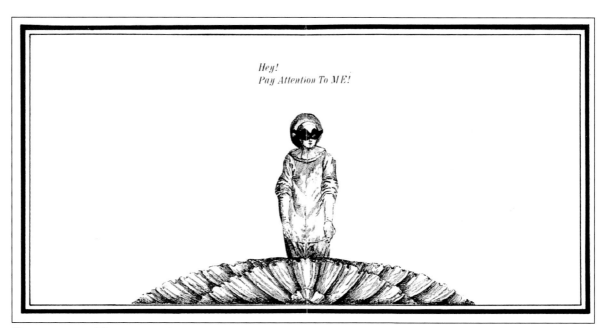

Hey!
Pay Attention To ME!

SUNSHINE
Card interior design by Sätty

SPACED
Sätty

GEODISIC ROSE
Sätty

TEMPTRESS
Sätty

THE VAST HEAVEN IS OPEN
Sätty

ALPHA
Mary Wagner

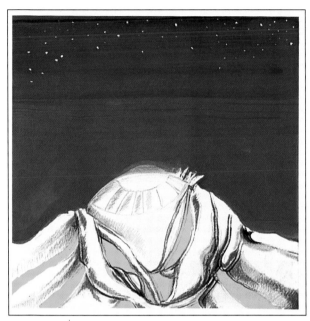

OMEGA
Mary Wagner

BIBLIOGRAPHY

Albright, Thomas. *Art in the San Francisco Bay Area, 1945–1980: An Illustrated History.* Berkeley: University of California Press, 1985.

Ferlinghetti, Lawrence, and Nancy J. Peters. *Literary San Francisco.* San Francisco: City Lights and Harper & Row, 1980.

Gleason, Ralph J. *The Jefferson Airplane and the San Francisco Sound.* New York: Ballantine, 1969.

Graham, Bill, and Robert Greenfield. *Bill Graham Presents.* New York: Doubleday, 1992.

Grogan, Emmett. *Ringolevio: A Life Played for Keeps.* Boston: Little, Brown, 1972.

Javna, John, and Gordon Javna. *60s!* New York: St. Martin's, 1983.

Lee, Martin A., and Bruce Shlain. *Acid Dreams: The CIA, LSD and the Sixties Rebellion.* New York: Grove Press, 1985.

McDonough, Jack. *San Francisco Rock: The Illustrated History.* San Francisco: Chronicle Books, 1985.

Roxon, Lillian. *Rock Encyclopedia.* New York: Grosset's Universal Library, 1971.

Sätty. *The Cosmic Bicycle.* San Francisco: Straight Arrow Books, 1971.

———. *Time Zone.* San Francisco: Straight Arrow Books, 1973.

Stevens, Jay. *Storming Heaven: LSD and the American Dream.* New York: Harper & Row, 1987.

von Hoffman, Nicholas. *We Are the People Our Parents Warned Us Against.* Chicago: Quadrangle, 1968.

Walker, Cummings G., ed. *The Great Poster Trip: Art Eureka.* San Francisco: Coyne & Blanchard, 1968.

Wolfe, Burton H. *The Hippies.* New York: Signet, 1968.